Scream

A Collection of Poems

Edited by
Jewels Johnson

EditRed

First published in Denmark in September 2007 by
EditRED

Copyright © 2007 by EditRED

ISBN 978-0-6151-6445-8

EditRED
Dybbølsgade 14, st. th
1721 Copenhagen V

www.EditRed.com

To the people who introduced me to my first love – poetry. And all those whose words will leave me in awe, and resonate with me forever.

Contents

Foreword

by Jewels Johnson

The first poem I read was when I was a little girl of seven in a poetry anthology given to me for Christmas in 1977, it was 'Rain' by Shel Silverstein and it went like this:

I opened my eyes
And looked up at the rain
And it dripped into my head
And flowed into my brain
And all that I hear as I lie in my bed
Is the slishity slosh of the rain in my head.
I step very softly
I walk very slow
I can't do a handstand
I might overflow

So pardon the wild crazy thing I just said.
I'm just not the same since there's rain in my head.

It injected such a quick fix of joy into me that I knew it was an experience I wanted to have again. It wasn't something that I could explain in words but something that made me feel something intensely. I felt like it was my very own discovery, a kind of magical treasure accessible only to me. This fix is something that I've continued to search for and satiate throughout my life. Poetry has become an essential part of my life, an addiction, my passion and friendship with it has continued to grow over the years. Both reading it and writing it has been my best friend and counsellor and helped me to survive the tough times life often throws at us. It has also helped me to learn what love is really about and that it is possible to express it through the beauty of poetry.

When I was asked to edit the EditRED poetry anthology, I was filled with a mingling sensation of excitement and apprehension. As the poems began to flood in I embarked upon a journey that frequently left me in awe. I felt like I was beginning an expedition, a kind of anthropologist excavating minds. The more catacombs I opened the least certain I became of what to expect.

I began my search for poems for the anthology with various expectations in mind. I hoped to be able to find poems that people can relate to in the world we live in today, poems that would reach as wide as possible an audience. As the Columbian poet José Asunción Silva says of poetry, " a poem is a holy vessel; put in diluted thought in it, only that- in whose blinking drop images gleam like the gold bubbles in an old, shone wine.
Thus our brutish existence is made sweet- as if with an unfathomable essence- burning in the flames of our affected souls: one drop of such matchless balm is enough".

A really resplendent poem should take all the little ingredients of our daily existence and filter through words that once may have seemed mundane transforming them into an enchanting and unforgettable pick and mix. Poems can often be like a hybrid between a pharmacy and a sweet shop, we dip into our bag of pick 'n' mix and are surprised by the flavours that linger with us; while at the same time they can often touch upon feelings we find cathartic. I held as my measure poets that have long remained friends on my bookshelves, Sylvia Plath and Ted Hughes. When I was 12 years old I read my first Sylvia Plath poem and the effect it had on me was profound. She managed to truly capture the bittersweet nature of life and the extremes from which she wrote were surprising, intoxicating and exhilarating. It made me realise the intensely vivid effect that poetry can have on a person and that it didn't always have to be about empathy but could sometimes be about providing a post mortem of events at the scene of a word explosive car crash. After reading Lady Lazarus, I felt I had been given a microscopic intricate glance into her soul, for which I felt privileged.

Dying is an art,
Like everything else, I do it exceptionally well.
I do it so it feels like hell.
I do it so it feels real,
I guess you could say I've a call

[…]

Herr God, Herr Lucifer,
Beware
Beware
Out of the ash,
I rise with my read hair,
And I eat men like air

So, with this is mind I hoped to find similar gems. Since first encountering Sylvia Plath and Ted Hughes, I have bought numerous poetry anthologies; hoping to find that same spine tingling soul nurturing, mind stimulating fix. Until this point I have been left feeling as though I have been browsing the shopping malls with plenty of money but little inclination to buy.

However I can make, what might seem to some the bold claim, that in this anthology, the reader wont be left feeling short-changed, as every single poem in 'Scream' will reveal the same glimmer of light as the catacomb is opened and voices are heard for the first time.
Some of my favourite lines from the anthology are:

I fear I could stand
(glasslike)
for years
watching for an expression.
I guess this
is what they call depression;
this eclipse of me.

                              -Sophia Argyris

Dog eared like an ancient scroll
Fragile and torn
The scars of time they score my skin
Always folded on the floor
Cant open up to begin
The sinful sores
Integrate with my pores
I'm agitated
Cant get on all fours

                              -Steven Hand

Your lips cold would kiss my
warm pillow creased cheek,
before mischief finds freezing hands
playfully running on my bare chest.
Forcing me from my foam
and feather lined haven.

Just one more secret embrace,
one more winter visit
would be enough.

                              -Dan Beck

What can you expect from Scream?

To uncover new voices and to bring poetry kicking and screaming into the 21st Century. An introspection into voices that reveal the diversity of the world we live in now, wherever that may be and to speak about feelings and thoughts that are both universal and -un-universal. Although many of us love classic poetry, to many it seems alienating; we want it to speak to us in a language we can understand.

The general consensus of many publishers is that people don't want to read poetry anymore. Poetry has been simply written off, buried away abruptly, and canonized with those classic poets of the past. Voices of new poets, buried with them in their tombs. I want to unearth these muffled voices and create a choir of buds blooming, new and exciting, alternative voices. Poems that tell us what it is like to be human and the myriad of feelings that go with this in a current and fresh way.

Writing that will make us feel electrified at one moment, so that our skin feels edgy and then pacified and womb-safe at the next. Poetry that can make us feel alive and then terrorises us with the pain of another being. "Scream" will help us feel what it is like to be mortal, exhilarating us with the joy or the mortality that entails. These poems will help us show how complete we can feel and then next sticks us in the washing machine on spin cycle, reminding us that being human isn't always about togetherness but also about being fragmented and different. Feelings that stick out on the page like a broken bottle, ready to make ourselves or another bleed at any moment. Poems that will pick at the scabs, hurts and happy of life but, somehow by reading them provide us with the plaster to make them all better.

Scream will take you on a journey of current times, the now, in times that we struggle through and rejoice, in poems that will not only reflect this but enable you to embody them briefly.

When you disembark from 'Scream' you will feel that your emotions have been exercised and exorcised and that you will have been to places that you want to revisit again and again.

Jewels Johnson
Colchester, June 2007
EditRed

The Dark

by Jewels Johnson
www.editred.com/Jewels

We go to places in our heads,
unseen by others.
Uncharted territory
we keep them hidden
to others forbidden
secret from our lovers
but incessantly linked to ourselves,
for, inwardly, our beasts dwell.
They are hairy and unsightly
and they yowl and scratch away
beneath our skin
they try to maul their way out
from our within
while we cover their mouths
with a threatening hand
muffled yelps vindicate their sound
restless, clambering, multi-limbed
the keepers of our secrets
custodian of our sins
when we sleep, they terrorise
when our daily routine is switched off
they still intervene
eating away at our nerves
sapping, lapping away at our energy
we resolve to stifle the enemy.
Though, in certain light
or particular sight

circumstances cannot reconcile
what comes from within
unveils itself without
and we catch its profile.

Feeling Autumn Today

by Mercedes Dawson
www.editred.com/TequilaTwilight

I am made of leaves,
veined and aged in seasons
where I have learned to fall,
a spiral that heads straight down
and I stay crumpled and stood on,
a mess on the floor.

Bad Day at The Canal

by Sara Pascoe
www.editred.com/sarapascoe

Lonely little fish,
Sitting on a bench
Looking at the Ducks on the water.
A mirror ripples by
And reflects the cloudy sky
And all the willows weep ever after.

Lonely little smile,
Drinking in the bench
And laughing at the Man's stripy jumper.
Too fat to float I think
Some fish were born to sink
To hide at home, from the couples and the Winter.

Stupid little cow,
Blinking at the bench
As the music of the Mews passes by her.
Tired eyes are getting cold
Ducks in jumpers sail the world
Smoke Drink Move on with world on shoulders.

Moonface

by Sophia Argyris
www.editred.com/Sophia

Moonface
Life like, life less;
I'm unsure which is me.
A mirror held up
does no more than reflect
an emptiness.
Restful,
(in repose I suppose),
no emotion lifts this face
from apathy.
I fear I could stand
(glasslike)
for years
watching for an expression.
I guess this
is what they call depression;
this eclipse of me.

The First Goodbye

by Nick Linde
www.editred.com/ nlinde

The First Goodbye
her face appeared to be broken
from age old concrete.
A life that spanned generations
reduced to a plastic bag
slowly dripping lunch in
the form of liquid memories,
each splash, each breath,
taking one more sepia image away.

Her lucid glare moved without effort
from the monitored hourglass
to a tilted frame hanging on the wall.
Her eyes met a younger shell of herself,
the stare seemed to dissect a dimension
only known to the half-living.
Each breath excruciating, as a slow
deliberated move in a chess match.

Her ice blue eyes, oddly clashing
with her ghostly skin, close tensely
as she parts her lips and lays
her hands, palm down, onto the pillow top
mattress. Awaking again only
to blow the image of herself one last
kiss before exhaling and watching
the last drop fall from the tube.
Checkmate.

Make Me Sepia

by Sophia Argyris
www.editred.com/Sophia

Last night, lost in darkness,
I dreamt of signalling with blinds
across an empty street,
signing distress in silence
while the world stayed asleep.
An atmosphere of desperation
sunk like varnish into wood;
the house felt more than empty,
more than hollow.

Looking at old photographs
where colour never dared
brighten and enliven eyes,
or warm cheeks with a flush of red,
I wonder if I could have found
more peace in shades of grey.
Softer than the raucous crowd
splashed across the walls today,
vying for attention.

Shrieking at the Sky

by Scott Harris
www.editred.com/Harris3dgn

Stab straight up
You'll hurt your wrist
Leap at shadows
And you'll hit a wall
Stub your toe
And blame God(s) for the offence
Fire a gun into the night
Eventually the bullet falls

Staring straight up will only
Hurt your neck
Shrieking at the sky
Will only make you hoarse
Level heads and levelled eyes
are what you need to chart your course.

Let the stars be
Leave the God's alone
They just want you to do it on your own

Because wings don't grow on men
And oceans don't part for them
Shrieking at the Sky
Will only make you hoarse.

Frustrations at 23.33

by Colin Williamson
www.editred.com/Midden

A relentless thief,
the clock snaps on
staring ahead
Ignoring the fear.

Spilled from below,
a cool yellow glow.
The people pause
for an answer.

Marching us on
an undead drill instructor,
our life is a pawn,
our minds become their shelters.

I hate your cold echo,
your definite chime.
I hate your blank face,
your mask of pretension.

I nurse in your shadow,
your voice rules my essence.
But I hate you untold,
inside I murder you with pleasure.

Dreaming of Drowning

by Sophia Argyris
www.editred.com/Sophia

When the nightmares crawl behind her eyes
and anguish leaves its thumb print just below them,
a little scratch is nothing.
The fuel that keeps this fire burning
could engulf a world.

Skin's too thin to protect, too weak to hide behind;
you need armour and weapons to fight.
Madness is the pit, the ocean;
she hovers at its edges,
tempted to jump off if things get tough –

to dive into depths where only blueness breathes.
It may be safer there where sound is drowned,
the walls padded with seaweed
and all sharp objects dulled by the
inability to make sudden movements.

Living underwater would be gentler than this

Caged Bird

by Jewels Johnson
www.editred.com/Jewels

I hide my eyes
so you cannot see
the pain
that curls up
inside of me
clenched like a fist
I relent in your cold grip
and there is stillness
and there is vacancy
silence
where before you had unleashed
a million dancing butterflies
swirling
fluttering
inside of me
careful not to tear their wings
on jagged edges
amongst my broken dreams
there was singing
it reverberated
throughout me
caught
my breath
when I opened my mouth
a nightingale flew out
Your song
your beauty
entwined itself

around my veins
like the strongest oak
taking up root
with the promise of forever
eternity
but now my torment chokes me
a clinging ivy
and I am suffocating
under a heavy pillow of loss
for you.
Torture is the price I pay
for the orchestra of sunbeams
you once shone into my soul
the strings are broken
your love was just an interlude
intro
no outro
and only sorrow sings inside me now
there is a lump in my throat
it's the dead bird you caged
when you took your love away.

Paid Slave

by Shea Garrity
www.editred.com/sheabile

Work kills,
paid slave labour;

9 to 5
– Prescription suicide.

Like,
down-staged hanged man
mouth-taped,
silent on the mic.

Dance in place,
work for pay.

Trot by day,
die by night.

Like,
comp screen
wears the SS,
trading your soul windows
for dollar sign
eyelets.

God damn,
switch to Plan ME.

But can't,
holy Green Man
cuts the check.

Like,
Jolly Nazi
got me shooting sheep
ass-backwards.

451°
– Watching a day's work

burn away the day dreams.

In a Box

by Nicole Hester-Francis
www.editred.com/NicFran

Four sides they say-is a box
Congruent and equal each side
Its dimensions and depth amuse me
Folding into a foetus, simple in mind

I want to emerge a-new
Trapped I am
Within these dimensions
A prison so true

Memories that must be fake
Drowned my dreams of sight
Playing around inside this box
A view-master of false thoughts
Flash the horror show within
Wearing me thin….

Hands and knees, now one

There is sometimes hope
It lets me see a flinch of light
A slight glimmer among faceless shadows
In a box…I am gripped tight

If I Had a Million Years

by John Arthur
www.editred.com/Kerosene

If I had a million years,
I'd build the ultimate cage.
It'd house every living insect,
And with it, all my rage.

I would send the cage away,
Postmarked First-Class.
To a place like Jupiter or Saturn,
To gag on hydrogen gas.

When the bugs were all gone,
I'd know my plan was perfect.
I'd finally enjoy summer,
And everything with it.

I'd have a barbeque in peace,
Sip soda by the pool.
Without being bit by gnats,
And horseflies so cruel.

One day those bugs might come back,
Perhaps a billion years later.
One hundred and fifty feet tall,
With minds even greater.

"We want to talk to the man,
the one who shipped us through space.
We will hunt the scum down,
and chew off his human face."

I know I'd be dead,
Unless I found some protection.
In a world taken over,
By my Unnatural Selection.

Bulletin Bored

by Corey Evans
www.editred.com/flypaper

We've signed on to these various blogs, groups, and chats.
We spend all night hunting for the right avatar Photoshop hack.
We must appear to be interesting, always writing something cool,
Hey look! I can make the screen jump with these hi-tech communication
tools.

Just imagine this repeating, in all nations worldwide.
Often we will come here to escape and to hide,
Our thoughts travelling through air, wind and wires
in this vast network of critics, thieves, and liars.

Bitter Sweet

by Lahana Mysteria
www.editred.com/LahanaMysteria

I am bittersweet in this strange setting,
of left behind,
riding the wings of,
good luck and goodbye.

You have poisoned my fruit,
with leaves of green envy,
unable to feel this moist,
tear soaked earth beneath,
my blanket of blind love.

She has crept into my dream,
stolen my memories,
crashed and burned,
my hollowed out thoughts.

I can't hurt you,
make you feel tormented,
dejected,
as I have,
time for me goes forward,
backward,
but never close to what matters to you most.

You have me,
I hate you,
she alone is yours to possess now...

I fear,
this strange and bittersweet setting,
alone with my thoughts,
and cold revenge waiting to be served.

Clay

by Gabrielle Faust
www.editred.com/gsfaust

I am clay; ☐Bits of vertebrae
And squandered breath,
Pressed down between
The stones and molten
Legacy of our ancestors,
Dredged from the quarries
And passed into artisan hands
To be worked and pressed,
Inside out by calloused
Skilled fingers,
Fixed yet spinning,
Transfixed and yielding,
Till the magnetic fingerprint
Of the Universe is forever engrained
Within my refined and humming core
By the purifying kiss of a flame.

I am clay;
Whose hollowed painted body
Now holds water
From the well spring,
Running swift in
Its ancient carriage to the sea,
Beneath the meadows for eons,
Upon which the woman
Walks with me,
Perched perilously graceful
Upon her ample swaying hips,

Before she brings my
Imperfect mouth to her lips,
To rinse clean the
Residual impurities
And regrets from her body,
As the sun sets on her destiny,
And her dreams.

I am clay;
To be shattered without remorse
By the wrath of War,
Beneath hooves of
Smouldering enslaved solider horses,
And buried deep,
Entangled with the bleached bones
Of their enemies,
To be forgotten
In shimmering snow banks
And lush monsoon rains,
Under the rise and fall
Of grasslands and empires,
Till the whisper of history
Tugs gently at one human's curiosity
To dig down to the darkness
Where my dormant life force
Still gently hums.

I am clay.

Van Dream

by Corey Evans
www.editred.com/flypaper

Back in Spanish Harlem,
With trees swinging,
Ringing the bells.
Soaked by another rain.

Sweaty people
On a steamy bus
In the downtown core
"I'm cored out man"
Says the leper off hand.
"Off with her head" and grins,

And the gap is black
Where blue teeth have been before.

Now is the time to score,
But not to win.

Bicycles break,
as do the roads they ride on,
But they keep on being,
Cycling.

Face after face,
An endless sea.

Glare, cold stare
stimulation, titillation,
Burning chrome hornets eating advertising.
Hastings and Main.

Nothing of Value in this Car

by James Gormley
www.editred.com/JamesGormley

"Nothing At All of Value in this Car"
The sign proudly proclaimed in inch-high type
As I passed down a street in The City.
But what of the dreams you packed in your bags?
And of the hopes you folded so neatly
In the trunk in ordered Midwestern squares.
Yes, what of the dreams you packed in your bags

Coronet of Ash

by U.V. RAY
www.editred.com/U.V.RAY

Returning to the city
of 20 years before,
the street no longer throbs
with that old familiar cadence;

no longer swings to the beat
of rent boys and pimps –

the titty bars are gone

the triple XXX cinemas

and all the old dance clubs
have closed.

Now austere faces
stare from the glimmering facades
of pseudo-suave
cosmopolitan bistros
where the music is turned down low
and the precincts resound
to the brutal sound of pneumatic drills
as they bulldoze the buildings
and tear up the pavements
the hookers once cruised.

The heart of this town has died
and you can hear
the crack of its bones
as the cement of its past
crumbles like a coronet of ash
upon the broken skull
of a pawn.

Withered

by Steven Hand
www.editred.com/misplacedmind

I'm looking in the mirror
I'm withered and worn
Dog eared like an ancient scroll
Fragile and torn
The scars of time they score my skin
Always folded on the floor
Cant open up to begin
The sinful sores
Integrate with my pores
I'm agitated
Cant get on all fours
I'm discombobulating
I search for the cure
I take what's on your plate
Only state words when its pure
Minutes like seconds
Brush fast past our eyes
Innocence in our expressions
We are a similar size

The Subway

by James Gormley
www.editred.com/jamesgormley

Subterranean beasts of burden whisk
Human vessels under The City's streets.
Full of colour-bursting passions, dreams, tears
Well-sealed with drab coverings of boredom.
I must trust your sudden fascination
In my umbrella. Her cane. His paper.
As you look at your watch, I look at mine.

We All Fall Down

by Dee Toth-Jones
www.editred.com/Scarlett

Wear a pretty dress, like Mummy does.
Curl your hair, like Mummy does.
Bake the bread, like Mummy does.
And we'll all fall down.

Go to work, like Daddy does.
Drive the car, like Daddy does.
Win the bread, like Daddy does.
And we'll all fall down.

Sleep alone, like Mummy does.
Sleep around, like Daddy does.
Cry alone, like Mummy does.
And watch your world fall down.

Shh

by Robert James Egan
www.editred.com/rjaye21

Shhh?…
Listen, there is no sound.

Constant grind & whine of metal against metal now ceased.
As the liquidated remains of our tropical, submerged history expire we
lament for a new reserve.
The black upon black,
the legacy of centuries burned,
our subservience to luxury and the modern.

Comfortable, climate adjusted rooms and automobile,
fast paced, unwavering time-scale with a 2 day turn-around from the far
east jet wash.
Clouds present little more than a lull in the violence of the sun after
layers removed,
our lives forever filled with regret,
how we were told, how we were warned, how we selected inaction &
opposed,
prefer our subservience to luxury and the modern.

Baked in ever increasing Celsius, the parched remains of great wooded
hills blow dust in the dry breeze,
we inhaled, our lungs now filled with the effluent of incessant industrial
progress & motion,
we choked, eventually.
How green once was, now replaced with dulcet earthen tones and arid
vastness,
reduced to screen viewed recordings from more fertile memories,
resent out subservience to luxury and the modern.

Fuck It

by David Dannov
www.editred.com/daviddannov

In the last few years,
I've been trying to find a publisher
for my poetry manuscripts.
I've got three of them, each 300 pgs.
Yesterday, I was at it again. I looked online
and found hundreds of independent
publishers.
I was excited. After scanning
the many books of poetry
that they published, however,
reading a few excerpts of the authors' poems,
I realized
I didn't have a chance.
They wanted University professors,
safe words in a safe world.
* A biochemist wife.
* An award winning poet
who told yawning stories
without a single cuss word.
None of it spoke to me.
Not a word: nature poetry talking about gardens
and flowers and crap.
Even at the bookstore,
after perusing through
the poetry section,
I found the same cowardly
yammer of words.
One of these poets

sacrificed their lives for their poems.
Only Charles Bukowski shouted through
the bookshelves.
He gave it all up
for the poem,
lived in ratty hotel rooms,
worked shit jobs,
became a drunk:
a bloody lion
fighting
against everything boring
and sterile.
Compared to Charles,
the rest of them wrote like
five-year olds
hiding
behind their mother's skirt.
They were afraid of offending someone.
Afraid to say cunt.
Afraid to confess
Their dirty little lives.
Afraid to live without
having dental care.
And there they all were
being published
as if they were
the heroes
of our time.
Even the photographs of these poets
sickened me.
One man sat on a front stoop
wearing a 500 dollar suit
with a yellow tie
and black, shiny shoes.
What could this man possibly teach me?
I thought, considering

I lived in a cockroach-infested studio,
watering plants
to survive.
All I could do
was sit on the rug of the book store
and shake my head
and laugh.

The Vulture

by Steven Hand
www.editred.com/misplacedmind

The vulture of the drug culture
I get my claws in deep
The silent one that creeps
When you're all asleep
The emotional motions
At the crest of the peak
Our confessional speech
Leaks as we speak
The damage irreversible
The price for unique
Personality deleted
For the rest of the week
The next time we confer
Ill be hard to reach
Come fly in my world
Its my time to teach
Ill set by example
Give in to my disease
Let your body dismantle

Curly Locks and Smiles

by Dan Beck
www.editred.com/Beck

Curly locks and smiles
you hide in my corner and cupboard,
covering mouths with hands
to smother the sniggers.

Sneaking while I sleep,
you siphon
fiery lights that
sing in my belly 'til
morning.

Persistently hungry
I allow to feed
a parasite
a memory
and truth…

…missing you feeds the fear I will forget that missing you is all that
matters

Goldfish

by Jewels Johnson
www.editred.com/Jewels

In the sad still mist
of the foetal dawn
it's not you
whose lips I kiss.
But the willing stranger
who promises to erase
all memory of you.
and be all that you are not
yet as the stale stench of guilt
hangs heavy in the air
above what only moments before
had masqueraded
as love.
It reveals itself to me again
like a smiling assassin.
The highway man
of all moral vows.
The stranger
an empty vessel
that had carried my salacious
appetite for you as its passenger.
The convenience food that leaves
a hollow rocketing echo
and constantly fails to be
You.
The wall I deliver myself to.
The available
when you

are unavailable.
I claim again my consolation prize.
Like a goldfish at the fair
staring at me with empty eyes
that appear soul-less.
And its short term memory
just enough
for me to return
and be fooled again.

Blissful Denial

by Dan Beck
www.editred.com/Beck

Unswerving bullet
from your breath,
leave your scratching tongue to rip a seam.
I will seal the cracks without hate.

Savour the taste
I shall not linger,
for fear my running fingers swallow your skin
in search of hidden secrets.

For now
I will keep you…

… and smile.

When the bliss begins to creak
I will oil your parts and keep you clean.
False for you for me a dream

A Paranoia Lingers

by Dan Beck
www.editred.com/Beck

Have you ever felt the sun were a spy
hiding in its burning brightness
waits an army of fireflies
ready to swallow your skin
and soul in an outcry of flames.

Have you ever seen the night as a plague
darker it becomes
and further it spreads,
gargantuan its hunger
and will to devour everything.

Have you ever held a lover's heart in your hands
awestruck by its gentleness
and overpowering beauty
bathing in tears so splendid
they caress the senses.

There is nothing more dangerous than this.

Close your fist.

The Girl Who Swam Through a River of Bees

by Mike Snowdon
www.editred.com/LittleMike

There was a young girl from Gloucester,
Who swam through a river of bees.
The winged, furry insects did sting her!
In particular, they aimed for her knees.

When she came to the end of this river,
The girl hauled herself out with a groan.
And as she slowly looked back with a shiver,
She realised she was now alone.

For all of the bees had now stung her,
And soon after bees sting you they die.
So the river was now a bee graveyard.
And the girl could do nothing but cry.

Untitled

by Samantha McQuillen
www.editred.com/SamiJo

You came to me one night
You stole into my dreaming wakefulness
And raped my sanity
You looked so familiar to me
Yet your namelessness
Ate at my emptiness
The sorrow you beat me with
Filled me with clarity
I know you
Your impoverished essence
Makes my peacefulness wealthy
The blackness that follows your footsteps
Smells of ancient decay
Yet it is as perfume from the garden of the eternal
To speak your name just once
Would be a symphony of razorblades

Fucked Bad Luck

by Lana Burke
www.editred.com/history

all this screaming music
can't be good for me
it's burning my meaning
any reasons
I had for breathing
are being scorched
away
into my arms with cigarettes
smoking, slow choking
suicide is exploration
of the unknown
100 things to do before you die,
love, lose, hate, thrive, drink, hate, die
boredom the only something
I still feel
no more numbness
scars don't heal quick
enough
blackness is
so
comforting
a womb filled with vodka
a manic's ideal
of
emancipation
poor self-image
microcosm
dissected

elected to be
see yourself celebrity
dead raped cells no less
a sobbing, weeping mess
of who the fuck knows
repressed?
the reason you're depressed?
no I don't think so
just a soul with too much to go
too much too know
thinking
always thinking
no distinction
between what you see
and what you should be
I know
It's fucked
Bad Luck

If

by Rabab Khan
www.editred.com/rabableo

If life were a curtain
would you hide with me
behind the dark folds,
away from red-eyed you?

If life were a desk
would you help me
put away my fears,
in the deepest drawer?

If life were a classroom
would you expect me
to solve wisely
all the difficult questions?

If life were real
would you try me,
as each day you do,
for every mistake?

If life were my own
Would you grudge me
even that bit,
what little is there?

Morning Wrath

by Isobel Edment
www.editred.com/izzye

Oh god, there's that sound again
My heart races, pounding deep within my chest,
Watching the colours of my dreams disperse,
Leaving in their wake a watery grey gloom.

Please, just a wee while longer.
And I hit the snooze before the words fall to the ground.
Lying in a place between the waking and the dead,
It is so warm, comfortable and pleasantly addictive.

Fearing the day and wondering with dread, just what it might bring.
I can't seem to move; there must be something wrong.
As I dry a few stray tears from eyes,
The final call, rings in my ears.

Sleepwalking through the necessary tasks,
Thinking the most profound thoughts;
What has become of us and the world?
With the sharp taste of mint in my mouth
I SPIT.
Dressing in clothes that I hate and despise,
forgetting all of the things that I promised I would do.
I grab my coat
And start to run, I'm late.

Legs aching,
Cold and wet.
Walking the path that has worn my shoes thin.

Not seeing anything that I pass, I am blind,
Blind to the world.
I finally make it to the steps
And I just want to turn and run as I see all those faces
Faces that I recognise, but have never met.
Nameless suits litter my view, and that familiar feeling of insignificance
sets in.

Waiting in the rain,
To go somewhere I don't want to be.
It feels like forever and a day before the train clatters up to the platform.
As I climb aboard my ride
The sun begins to shine.
Warming me with its rays,
Like a knife in the back.

I walk to the same seat,
Next to the same ghostly face
Avoiding all eye contact,
As the train begins to pursue the tracks.
Muted colours flash past in a blur.
Through towns so derelict and nondescript,
Full of faces with no names.
Wishing my life away,
As I race towards the end;
The colours come to a stop,
This is the end for me,
My sentence begins.

As I willingly walk to what seems like my death,
For a few small pennies to buy
A few small essentials,
To feed that commercial, consumer monster.
Welcome to the cage,
Get comfortable and become blind.

Sudden Drop

by Amanda Walczesky
www.editred.com/Manda

a vivid mixing
ether flux and shadow shifting
sense of falling
failing
tethered to poisonous cilia

hijacking gravity
you deepen the spiral
plummeting
uninterrupted eternity
atoms burst, pops of light
shredded presence
as you descend

an abyss gouged into
the purity of time
the blackness slowly bleeds
off the edges of
your ebbing
mind

The Alzeimer's Poem

by Paul Coman
www.editred.com/Violet_Blue

Dying is an art –
here the ribbons of old film are unfurling,
like the black trail of an umbilical cord
seeking out its dead mother.

You are standing on the station,
immovable by the sluggish moon-boots of illness.
Awaiting death's kindly killing, or the arrival of your
own screaming foetus; neither come except the usual sycophantic court.

They all claim to know you: Brothers, sons and grand-children.
Yet they do not understand your new language –
a Morse code of helplessness and rage.
The signals are released, but no one is receiving.

Shapeless now, existing in space and time only;
yet not knowing what time and space is.
The gutless white coats administer pharmaceutical justice,
but the pills don't send you to Alice's wonderland.

Anarchy of the mind is the greatest form of democracy.
However, it comes with the fascistic loss of identity.
You stare in the mirror with consummate concentration,
but all you get is a fiercer enemy staring back.

This insidious onset of cruelty,
a form of capital punishment for longevity.
The glass breaks (though you don't know how);
the enemy is still there, peering through the shards.

This tango with death will arrive one day.
Until then, comfort your withered mind with this knowledge for now:
That you never deserted yourself;
rather your self was taken from you.

Dying is an art –
you have already erased the fragile lines of familiarity.
Once the canvas is blank,
you can move on to your final memory.

Heavy Metal

by Judy Kaber
www.editred.com/jkaber

My heart is a magnet.
Each night I pull off
iron filings, paper clips,
safety pins. I touch a loose nut
to my tongue and taste
the bitter missing screw.
When I breathe,
exhaustion fills my lungs
like oil. I smell tungsten
burning in the light, feel
the heavy air pressing me.
Edison kissed me. Tesla slipped
me wires beside the Colorado.

Nothing sticks to my heart.
I sit on the tub and hold
my head. I've been right out
straight all day. Bruised my arms
carrying so much weight. You've got
to kick it with all your strength
to get the day rolling. The wrenching
grasp of time hangs in my clothes.
Each morning I try to pull
the right door open.

I hold my heart under the faucet
to ease the burn. Whisper songs
to quiet the yelling pain.

My lungs will burst, my engine won't ignite.
Open dust will fill my mouth like rust,
Copper vines will spiral round my ribs.
Birds make meals of piston rings and iron lungs.
Hors d'oeuvres bang madly on the table.
Forks tap tongs and dance impatiently.

I pin my nightgown shut
and smell the stew meat
burning in the dark.

Are we Different?

by Rabab Khan
www.editred.com/rabableo

The ones who won and
The ones who lost,
Can they be any different
from you and I?

Desire led them
as it leads us,
Greed moved them
as it moves us.

Are we different when we too
belong to those driven by
love,
hate,
right
and wrong?

The Lore of Living Lies

by Billie ThaKid
www.editred.com/billiethakid

Living lies thus multiply, then divide the mind's eye of their owners
Surreptitiously increasing, they're distinctively releasing noxious Toxins
within their donors
To their chagrin,
Fear lives within
An augmented, exclusively demented, overtly invented place of Internal
judgment
Causing rejuvenation, removing the devastation, but never full
Restoration of the broken covenant
Pensively stained with much disdain, yet clearly aimed aching hearts
Will tell a story
They importune mankind
And swear of truths with double sides
And hang the noose between the lines
Much of which is the lore of we.

For What it isn't Worth

by Meleina Backhaus
www.editred.com/waxseal

For what it's worth,
The Man might always win,
but the People have the last laugh.

The streets might clog with protests,
and fire might burn an eye,
but there will always be apple pie at Grans".

March to work
fight for food
kill for love (obsession)
die for fun

Run run as fast as you can,
fighting to be with the band,
running from the government
keeping your eyes behind you in case a paycheck catches up

Fuck the world I'm an American
but California can drop into the sea
The world is all one,
but everyone keep their problems to themselves

For what it's worth,
It's a sophisticated mess,
the press a dress for problems,
policy a crutch

Who needs the generation who doesn't know its name,
go back to our parents, Nixon had it figured out –
cheat our way to happiness, complain when it goes right

keep our enemies imagined,
so friends seem less dangerous,

Dream on Dream on Dream on
roll a cigarette at the no smoking sign
Find a time to tell a shadow of the truth,

and open your jaded story with
For what it isn't worth.

The Whiskey Crawl

by Colin Dardis
www.editred.com/colindardis

My throat has that whiskey crawl about it
when the ice is forgotten
and all the oesophagus feels
is the firewater burn
of beakers, containers,
test tube shots,
glass receptacles
pouring flames on a drowning man
until that man is engorged
in his own wanderings
of crazed, empty curiosity
not a lust, but
that can't-help-but-wonder bewilderment
on the stained disco floor,
a sad, desperate volume
that liquid will not fill.

Hearts are not fluid
and into the vacuum of valves and arteries
the whiskey crawl comes
to rebound echoes of previous nights
into the place
where a familiar comfort once rested
on the coals of Sunday mornings
when hangovers did not matter:
they were laughed at even,
the warm, coarse laugh of the whiskey drinker
after feeding off a few.

Biding Time

by Tom Gant
www.editred.com/Tom

Hooked on shoulder bones
he steps with sticks
his only other burdens
old age and a heavy camera
on the fragile frame

Still, alert and able
he glances around
searching
for somewhere to go
and something to put his lens to

I pass by,
sea blue eyes
up and down me
from behind a complexion
crumpled as paper
then tearing away
to search through the rest
of his surroundings.

Hair beyond grey
whitish halo purity
pausing
he unhooks the camera
to point steadily
at a bird on a turn-style
of the closed theatre

But before he shoots
it spreads wing
and flies away
unused
the camera is hooked back
onto failing bones

A mile or so down the road
I take the risk
of a glance backwards
and sure enough
see myself
fifty years forwards
old and alone
plain
and still searching
for something in this world
worth truly capturing

Like Stars to Earth

by John Arthur
www.editred.com/Kerosene

Tears dive to the floor,
shiny bombs from my face.
Like every star falling to earth,
a rain shower from space.

My mind is frozen,
the gear is stuck in neutral.
Locked in a grey world,
with an amorphous future.

The music has ended,
silence has swept the room.
Planted in a coffin,
that's prepared for two.

We will meet again,
a heavenly reunite.
But for now my friend,
goodbye and goodnight.

Just a Love Poem

by Robert Capps
www.editred.com/logicustracticus

Will I miss you yes, I will write less
I will fight less. Must if I must in my lust discuss,
how I want to kiss caress stroke and float emotive,
salivating in… pleasure,
From reading your words,
some absurd when first heard,
But in recollection, the inflection felt
on my vow vetted heart.

When starting to drift off to sleep,
thou keep me warm on cold nights.
The sight of that image… the homage I use as my view of.
What you look like as each night in your mirror your framed,
You may see a reflection beautifying end of the day.
But I see from the stars high in the sky,
refracted through dew on new moon
A mite of the sight that is bounced back to
Earth from gaseous space, a settling on
my fervent face earnest in prayer now consumed

But alas I can't feel or reveal my feelings: kneeling on my knees,
Praying to the gods that I will awake once again to explain with,
mere words combined and twined together, quilled by doves feather
Glowing with such purist of love, showing just how I treasure,
Your smile and your grace that's has been seen around this place,

All calm and serene like a scene from a dream or fantasy like a
phantasm or like that innovative orgasm organized disorder
Of body and soul my goal is to repay you in kind, so
If you find your self one night, at sixes and seven it is
Only me transporting you to the heavens, thanking you
For all that you've done, as so often you've stroked while
You smote this lonely heart of mine

Cool Front

by Lolly G
www.editred.com/Lolly

today the weather changed
from sweltering to breathable
more than breathable
amusement park weather
picnic in the park weather
today I remembered the look of peace
on my friend's face
not those little ravines in his mother's cheeks
I heard an "I love you"
whispered into my head

Bound

by Antonio Beardall
www.editred.com/menoh

The echoes of my dreams surround me
Warm like the sun,
Quick as the shadow
Obscured from light,
Bathed in the images and senses
That exists in the memory
That came from a dream
Inspired by you.

Your very touch
Your heat
Alive now
In a brain once quiet
And a heart once dead,
Resurrected
By the power of your being.

Songs become a temptress
Beckoning me
To surrender to you
And bestow my love
To grant my life,
To your honour,
Glorified before me.

My soul, a bound captive,
Paying tribute
To a god
Who stole me away

From earthly cares
And has shown me promise
Eternal

The Traveler

by Steven Hand
www.editred.com/misplacedmind

The traveler, the late night rambler
Out of town in the city
With my spiritual partner
I'm consumed by her character
Smell her essence
Her vapor
The night sky is stupendous
But her presence is greater
Your eyes are so wide
Bright and mindful
You yawn and sit aside
Even your sighs are insightful

My Soul in the Blender

by John Arthur
www.editred.com/Kerosene

my eyes bleed blue
when truth is said
words are like cotton candy
sweet inside my head

slabs of regret
fills up the weak
baskets overflowing with
rotting, stinking meat

you're precious, a
sweet lullaby
unlike myself;
spoiled eats and sugar treats
a perfect blend,
unified

Echoes

by Antonio Beardall
www.editred.com/menoh

Voices bouncing off the ancient walls,
The energies of the spirits around us,
Of days long gone in glory.
The sun shines again on this empty city
Struggling against nature to exist,
Defeated into shadows and whispers
Of kings who once ruled,
People who once rejoiced and worshipped,
And gods who were brutal and unkind.
The moon was once high on gods in smoke,
The rush of blood burning into ecstasy,
Now faded like the burnt out candle,
With nothing but charred rope and wax remaining,
To take us back to what once was.
And now the silent spirits and ancient stones,
Cooking pots and disturbed bones,
Tell a tale of doom and survival,
The story of love and hate and pride,
Musical notes once carried in the wind,
Returns to glory and spoken words.

Forget the Smoke

by Colin Dardis
www.editred.com/colindardis

cheap, rancid cigars
useless as a penny whistle,
steal the breath from my mouth
'til my teeth clasp a vacuum
and I cannot speak
I won't speak
I will let the coolness of the night speak for me
I will let its briskness
its darkness
whisper out the secrets I cannot let
will not tell
no, I would rather keep them close
to myself
and suckle on their life-force
while I expel this acrid, arid, smoke
this arachnid smoke,
translucent
yet deep with rancour,
crawling out from my mouth
on thin, whispery legs
from my drying lips
hungry for your kiss.

Did I ever tell you
that kissing was my favourite pastime?
I think I did
I believe I did.
I am hungry for the moisture of your kiss

the smooth, cool wetness
the tenderness, the finesse
that a good
well-crafted cigar
might just
temporarily
replace.

I am the Life that Kisses Death

by Niccole Segura
www.editred.com/nonalienabductee

I
am the leap across the abyss
and I
am the dive from the cliff and
I am the wrong move and I am the
stupid idea
and
I am the crazy risk
and I am the off-road.
I am the things you shouldn't do
and I am the mischief on your shoulder and I
am the insane surfers during the hurricane
I
am the Geronimo from the plane
and I am the BASE jumpers
at the top
of the highest
buildings.
I am not high enough but
I could be wrong
and I am the "let it all ride" and I am the
gambler and
I am the last-second dash and I
am the fast life,
the die young,
and the beautiful corpse.
I am the burning candle which I lit with a blowtorch and I am
the idiot.

I am the mad grin before the dangerous run
and I am the sick/wicked/twisted/bitching tricks. I am the
speed.
I am always the speed.
I am the wind that screams in your ear
as the rollercoaster drops
And I am the poking that pushes you into danger.
I am the horrible
(glorious)
voice
that sings of wonderful
(deadly)
deeds. I am the triumph over sky.
I am the life that kisses death
and runs away
laughing. I am
the joy right before impact, the breaking bones,
the scars, the reason
for the shaking heads.
I am the bad influences,
the girls and boys your parents-and I-
say that you should never
imitate.
I am the early death
I am the mocked accident and I am the ones
who prove their point.
And I am the money blown on idiocy and
I am the shallow thrill-seekers and I am
those that leave no mark
But.
I
am the bound into the unknown and I am
the human condition
and I am the need to fly and I am the
none-in-a-million chance that happens anyway.

I am the one dancing on the edge.
I am
I am
the jump----------

Angel of Dream

by Shannon Dunny
www.editred.com/Dunny

Angel of dream and shadow
Emblazoned upon my chest
My passion thus evoked
My poet thus confessed
The veil once part of me
She now casts down away
The delicate lines I finally see,
By the light of her new day,
of her arcing words
of her arching back
of her aching soul
of her breaking lack
Fingertips part trembling lips
Seeking hands find timorous hips
Devour me as time feeds on youth
Devour her as eyes rejoice in truth
It was with abandon always
Flames from blind antiquity burn our body's whole
Waters of kind divinity preserve our common soul
And away, away to Heliopolis, my goddess and I go
With an egg of myrrh to the green, green desert,
covered hence in snow

Away from the Cold

by Cheryl Marren
www.editred.com/alien

A dream:
like bright lights burning
through dark eyes;

a sickening, subsonic drone,
driving insanity without knowing
how

or why.
Too late,
like a sweet, seducing lily,

drawing scented pathways
to forbidden gardens,
no entry signs unseen.

Breathe.
Caught unawares
by a touching smile,

a sleepy kiss.
A moment, almost
of understanding,

passed away like midnight,
quiet and unobserved.
The heart has no words.

Settle for silence, bathed
no more in drifting memory's voice;
lengthy abstinence

from the window.
Continue
in sorrow.

Wait
for an invitation to come
away from the cold.

Rehearsing in the Dark

by Judy Kaber
www.editred.com/jkaber

At night the wild woman next door calls
names, pounds walls, hoards acorns
in a jar beside the bed. Cats slide
like cream against her legs. Her feet
gleam sleek and pink from dancing.
Horns honk below her window,
waking me and I watch her slit pillows,
shake feathers down, croon shady amber
tunes to men who wait in a cavalcade
beneath her. She skates through mirrors
and grins at my white retreating back.
In the morning I find her leaning
at my door, a dog eared smile,
tongue wet with orange marmalade,
oak leaf splinters tangled in her hair.

smoke Joni, smoke

by George Wood
www.editred.com/Georg_Wood

like a VAN GOGH before it's madness, I sit watching
the smoke dance about the NO SMOKING sign on the wall,
little thought to the heart I wear on my sleeve

amongst an army of dead, I fortify my spot at the bar,
the bartender attacks the frontline with a stiff drink,
the bottles behind him glisten in the blue light of the TV
shipwrecking the heart broken on the false promises
mixed in the spirits he orders up

the reaper reflects back at me off the redness of my glass
that stands guard against the onslaught of life waiting
on the outside of this local hotel bar

the hot embers at the tip of my fag light up
the last reminisces of life in my eyes

the lipstick at its base's the only vibrancy
I taste through the stale nicotine
that flavours the patrons romantic before my eyes

Dialogue

by Steven Hand

www.editred.com/misplacedmind

I'm affected by my defects
They fill my entirety
I feel a weak sense
A reprisal from sobriety
Expression leaves stress
A repressed reflex
Collections of negligence
I dissect my dialect
I try to forget
But I re-enact the acts
Genuflect
Give in to intellect
Speak at lengths
Our reasoning mends
We leave still as friends
I breathe through the pen

Spilled Ink

by Joni Ramos
www.editred.com/Joni_Ramos

absorb this ink of mine
drenched with every trickle
of my tincture

blot it dry if you must
contain my stain
even for a moment

longing to be
tinged, sustained
by your touch

liquid elegance
my satiated ink

has savoured you
untarnished

A Day in the Life of Greg, a Speck of Dust

by Mike Snowdon
www.editred.com/LittleMike

Greg is a speck of dust.
He floats along daily, never stopping.
He is ever so busy at the moment,
Trying to finish his shopping.

Metamorphosed Dreams

by Joni Ramos
www.editred.com/Joni_Ramos

to live just a while
on borrowed dreams
of coloured wings
filament of desire
wrapped around my cosset
I dare to flutter
one day soar
spun from unripe hues
shedding my past goodbye
a sudden spectacle
of dappled wings
awaits
my metamorphosed dreams
I fly

NAKED MEN

by Lolly G
www.editred.com/lolly

when NAKED MEN
are NAKED
they are
without defence

they are
there
all there

I see right through
those slender hips,
tight asses,
smooth chests
and lust-filled eyes

I see
them
I see those
NAKED MEN

Rain

by Isobel Edment
www.editred.com/izzye

Gentle raindrops
fall on our heads,
roll
down our cheeks
and over our smiles.

They explode
with joy as they
hit
the ground and
seep
into the earth
and into our strong roots.

Cleansing and life giving
those tears from heaven.
Yet when they fall,
it only seems to make us cry.

Wanderlust

by Trace Sheridan
www.editred.com/tcbswan

She dreamed of
Paris in spring
and summers in Prague
of a City of Bridges
and London fog
of autumn in Rome
and winters spent lost
in Costa del Sol
or la Côte d'Azur
but settled for
an apartment
in Kitty Hawk
across the street
from Mr. Pete's
Meat, Dairy, and Eats
right above the wash and dry
two doors down
from Kim Ja Lau's
studio for Hapkido
and Tae Kwan Do
because her home
is where you are.
And Paris can wait.

A Winter Embrace

by Dan Beck
www.editred.com/Beck

Stirring from the sound of your entrance
I would wake as you perch yourself,
impatiently sitting on my foot,
with coy, deliberate intention.
Excitedly spewing forth words
to separate me from my
cosy bear cave quilt.

Wrapping one arm around your waist
I would smile plying you with a single
kiss on the small of your back.
Forever a secret embrace
hidden by your snow dusted coat
and thick woolly jumper.

Your lips cold would kiss my
warm pillow creased cheek,
before mischief finds freezing hands
playfully running on my bare chest.
Forcing me from my foam
and feather lined haven.

Just one more secret embrace,
one more winter visit
would be enough.

Orphan Bird

by Jewels Johnson
www.editred.com/Jewels

This
what I feel for you
is immortal,
its eternal.
Goes beyond
any word
I hold it in my hand.
Like an orphan bird.
Feed it hourly
with my attention.
I nurture it
and its fragile beak
but it doesn't ask anything of me.
Though it opens and closes its beak
expectantly.
It is sad in its captivity.
It doesn't need anything.
But I want to give it
all I have.
Regurgitate it.
Saturate it.
Drown it
with all that I can give
to make it live.
Its warm heart beats
moss soft in my palm
I feel its heat
and our pulses

ticking in unison
as one clock's cog.
It is tiny
compared to my life-sized clumsiness
but I need it
more than it needs me.
I want to tell it
not to be afraid
we are in this together
for the long haul.
But it fidgets
like an agitated
jumping bean
my tight clasp
its trampoline.
Its feathers sticking
in desperation
my perspiration
and I wonder
if
I will be strong enough to release it
a little
not smother
its face under a pillow
of euthanasia.
But I know.
Yes I know.
If my little bird
I uncover
and let it go.
It will return to me
and grow.

Inarticulate

by Jewels Johnson
www.editred.com/Jewels

Inarticulate
Cut.
Locked shut.
Dictionary
Switched off.
Thesaurus
Betrayed
Means more than words.
Need a language upgrade.
Ridiculous
Inconspicuous
Gaze
Full beam.
Heart
Full steam
Ahead.
Indicator on.
Vocabulary
Gone.
Check mirror
Rehearse.
Reverse.
Babushka Doll
Conceals the core.
Speak
No more.
Edit.
Face says it.

Veins ingrained.
Blood stained.
Start
Open surgery
To the heart
Access
To words
Unheard.
Scissors
Scalpel
I've forgotten
The aplhabet.

Want

by Lana Burke
www.editred.com/history

I want love
I want someone
OBSESSED
With me
Who cannot dream
Cannot breathe
Without me
Who's everything
Who's every waking thought
Devout
To she who he
Loves Endlessly
SO Complete, Relentlessly
Never Ending
Senseless

All I want is everything
All you want is me

An Invitation

by Hayden C. Clear
www.editred.com/theclearing

Every night I hear maudlin music played
from a distance, or maybe two steps back.
Its strings are like a wonderful array
of stars that the skies now lack.
It sings right in front of me, but far away
waiting at the end of a cul-de-sac.
It's you, if not me, 'cause I never was
the very voice I hear of a latent lass.

Merry Heart

by Omotayo Olaoye
www.editred.com/Tayo

I'm lost in the city of joy;
And like a child that forgot his food
When his hands were upon his toy,
So I'm carried away in the mood.

When the hands are highly honoured,
They take the legs to Myrrh Mountain
And make the body's odour fill the world.

When the eyes are rightly coloured,
They bring tears from honey fountain
And place the heart on top of the world.

Like a rose smiling in the sun,
So is my life glowing in the Light;
In my belly the sweet rivers run
And my face speaks about the heart.

When We Were Young

by Peter Budvietas
www.editred.com/ThePenguin

When we were young, a long time ago,
I thought us old,
Sitting around, talking the talk
Arguing like we were bold.

There were rainbows then
And rose-coloured glasses
And wine to drink
Dreams to follow, yet time passes
Our bones are creaky,
Our blood runs slower
Hurts last longer
Our tolerance lower
Idiots abound
Promises just aren't
Situations determine
What should be apparent

And, now was so long ago
Some think we are old
Sitting around, talking the talk
Arguing like we were bold

Yet still I listen carefully
And sometimes I hear the old you and me
We're still here, and still
With the power to see
The changes we want come to be

So, let's have a drink
A Bailey's or from the Scots
Not to old times
Let's celebrate lots
The future's still there.
Bright and clear
Rainbows need chasing
Though farther now than near

The pair from so long ago
Don't do what they're told
Sitting around, talking the talk
And acting as if they were bold.

The Park

by Annmarie O'Connor
www.editred.com/annmarie

We watched the swans and said nothing.

I talked endlessly of how they reminded me of my
childhood, of Yeats, of my sisters, of how they
symbolised beauty, purity and elegant sadness
but said nothing.

We couldn't escape the fact of the matter
tangled in the whisper of a November breeze,
waiting helplessly to be released.

We walked further along amidst the rustle
of small animals scuttling through the
undergrowth and said nothing

- yet saying more than we ever could or ever would.

This Dream

by Jack Thomas
www.editred.com/jackthomas

This dream is so lifelike, so vivid, so real,
I can feel every touch, every kiss.
But of course in reality one cannot feel
So intense and such unbridled bliss.
So I move through this dream, in which your heart is mine.
In exchange, my heart offered to you.
And as each hour passes lives further entwine,
Until one is created from two.

In this dream nothing matters but time that we're near.
In this dream you make everything right.
For the feelings and efforts so very sincere,
Filling darkness with dazzling light.

Life revived to a heart, so protected and cold
From the trauma and pain of the past.
But this dream creates miracles apt to behold.
This dream evokes love, meant to last.
There's no caution in here, no confusion or pain.
This dream allows only what's good.
With a sense of extreme that's so hard to explain,
But so very easily understood.

I hope against hope that this dream will go on
And the feelings attached will stay true.
That from here every break of every dawn
Will have my heart belonging to you.

But dreams are just that, fleeting hopes within thoughts
Soon to pass as they fade from one's mind.
Always dreams must dissolve, matters not how hard fought,
Leaving only a trace to remind.

As I open my eyes, fighting hard to secure
All this dream has allowed me to feel.
There you are, and the reason this dream seems so pure,
For this dream's not a dream…it is real.

Morning Rain

by Tony Lopes
www.editred.com/TonyfromBenoni

It began like drizzled oil
The stomach grumblings of the low nebula
Heralding its pitter patter arrival
While dogs bolted for warm kennels and birds frolicked

Happy for some
Others lurking troll-like under sheltering bridges
People-shapes scattering with plastic over heads
Playing dice with screeching cars

The contrails of red lights leaving smears
On the puddled iron-lung freeway
While cars and trucks and taxis sway
And jiggle in a deathly rain-dance

Clearing away into a dust-free haze of mist
Clean and fresh and good tra-la-la
The heaven-soap rumbles along to water
Farmers lands and parched cattle

One would hope...

She Is...

by MeaLee Thomas
www.editred.com/ MEA_da_POET

Bobin heads to the beat, snappin fingers in the air...
she is...
swaying her big ol hips to the beat
she carries the sound of soul, the navy of blues...
the rhythm of R&B n those hips
she ignores the cat calls, the whistles of "come here mama...sit those hips
right here on this.."
fists...to the sky
closed are her eyes
she syncopates her rhythmic thighs to catch the syncopated beat and the
singer's catchy rhymes

To and fro
Back and forth
Side to Side...she sways those big ol hips...

High on another frequency unheard by you or me,
she rides
The off beat of salsa,
The down beat of hip hop,
Upbeat tempos swinging
She is ol skool like V-neck sweatered cats be-bop singing

The crescendoing jazz tunes will draw her in deeper
The billowing tunes and lovers croons will keep her here longer

Bobin heads to the beat,
snappin fingers in the air...

she is…
swaying her big ol hips to the beat
she carries the sound of soul, the navy of blues...
the rhythm of R&B n those hips

Those hips that hypnotize and make everyone recognize the down beat
swinging
Blue note singer singing
Foot tapping
Hand clapping music
Banging on the walls
Stomping feet down the halls kinda music
Latino-centric, Afro-centric , Cuban laced sounds
Ay Crumba, This Hip-Hop...Hood-Hop Salsa Mama getting down
2 Stepping for the name of music she sashays turning round and round

Everyone's eyes are on those gumbo thickened hips
Every man in that joint yelling out come and dance on this
She ignores them and fights the power, fists to the sky
Lifts up her skirt above her calves to get her groove jus' right
Music in her ears and music sparkling in her eyes.

She is the essence of the beat, the soul of the rhythm and the heart of the
sound
Bobin heads to the records spinning round, snappin fingers in the air...
she is Music.

The Eternal Embrace

by Leo Chasseur
www.editred.com/Esquire

Observe not the Soul parted from another
For in our separation do we love
A tryst of minds; Love unto a lover

See our minds enveloped in grace
As Devotion I fall from my life to you
As Life I dream your eyes; flourish,
the Eternal Embrace.

Up Through the Night

by Eric Schwartz
www.editred.com/schwartzcaster

Up through the night
waves cascade and break
on the edges of a life
restless, rippling tide pools
catching nuances of the light
baby breathe with me a while
breathe with me
up through the night

This is a ballad of heavenly creatures
not a chronicle of shadowy things
of restless, babbling Byzantine children
in places without light
I'm happy to say
in the dream holes of suburbia
we're moving
up through the night

We all shimmer in the evening
at the end the long, long miles
bodies at rest, looking their best
in the suburban sunset's twilight
evening supper smells
and bedtime prayers of children
all drifting
up through the night

Gentle, loving whispers
barely perceptible through the wall
hiding part of your life
from the other part
this is just for the both of you
bursts of joy
and the bedtime prayers of lovers
sifting through pillows and slipping
up through the night

Rain and breeze in the high leaves
distant train horn and traffic
air conditioner drone - body magic
broad brush strokes deeper than my sight
all the world's asleep
smiling in the suburban deeps
dreams all shooting
up through the night

This is a ballad of heavenly creatures
not a chronicle of shadowy things

Ethereal Collision

by Freda Veluz
www.editred.com/fredav

Under the blanket of the infinite sky,
I gaze at shining celestial bodies,
while thoughts of you invade my heart.

The wind kisses my neck
and calls out your name,
as tiny, infinitesimal beings up high
collide, shatter, and burn.

Oceans away,
enveloped by this blackness,
you stare at the same dark canopy above
as I trespass upon your burning soul.

Our thoughts shatter, collide, and melt
as dawn arrives,
leaving us satiated and breathless..
with nothing but failed words
that scream... I love.

Woman

by Freda Veluz
www.editred.com/fredav

Celebrate your beauty
and feel the wind
that propels you
to improbable goals

Stand on tiptoes
flitting and dancing
from cloud to cloud
on wondrous thoughts

Explore your mind
and find within
the joys of
your soul's priceless treasures

Celebrate your beauty
and be not ashamed
You are woman.
Mother of Earth.
Giver of life.
Celebrate. And be known

Music Box

by Nick Linde
www.editred.com/nlinde

The woman dances. Music
pouring out. Silence, then melody.
Not playing because we opened the lid
but because our hearts recalled those precious notes.

Winding harmony from an aged cube.
Whisper of my mother. Whisper
of my past. My daughter's smile, her white pearls
luminous, the sunshine of the song.

Echoes etched in a timeless moment.
The laughter fills our worlds, the sound
familiar, the sound of my
mother and me. With one

With one touch, it begins again. We wind the key
around, around. The music
plays, like a bridge between
then and now. Her fourth birthday. The room filled

with love; our futures seem infinite.
we love, we listen. Silence,
then melody. Our eyes fixed on the candles.
They are blown out, but the music keeps playing.

Perspectives

by Jenni Meredith
www.editred.com/wordsart

The sun is sinking
over another Friday afternoon.

I walk towards home;
passing the charity shop coffee house

where, through curved glass
I see today's recycled people

collected to chat about their yesterdays,
knowing their tomorrows hold so little.

I climb the hill towards the sea.

A February blackbird trills,
reminding me

I have seen no thrushes
from the North this winter.

Behind the funeral director's
a private ambulance,

too long for the allotted space,
forces me from my path.

The sky is blue for ever
over a quiet sea,

And I am just another dot
diminishing well before infinity.

Woman

by Steven Hand
www.editred.com/misplacedmind

Expand my parameters
Overstep my barriers
Meet the circumference of the surface
Surpass my diameter
I surface
Absolved from my destitution
Resolve my solution
I'm absorbed in you
Woman

Red Lights and Roses

by Jenni Meredith
www.editred.com/wordsart

Tuesday morning
dripped into the sea
cried all afternoon.

Dusk fell early.
Sit with me this night
and wait for silence.

night is never black.
It fills with flame, blue
sirens, red lights. And

roses mark the spot
where one life stopped. When
so many others

never seem to start
I wonder why that
one has touched their hearts.

Love Buzz

by Colin Williamson
www.editred.com/Midden

Hold my breath until I burst
just trying to keep the buzz.
Take this buzz out,
introduce it to friends,
hang in a gang.

Enjoying this buzz
like our first love.
Screwing it,
as it screws us.